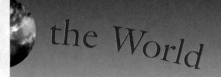
the World

The Italian Renaissance

Don Nardo

KIDHAVEN PRESS™

THOMSON

GALE

San ... leveland
Munich

THOMSON

™

GALE

Picture Credits

Cover Photo: © Erich Lessing/Art Resource, NY
© Alinari/Art Resource, NY, 34, 38
© Nicolo Orsi Battaglini/Art Resource, NY, 35
© Bettmann/CORBIS, 27
© Giraudon/Art Resource, NY, 5
Chris Jouan, 8, 10
© Erich Lessing/Art Resource, NY, 11, 14, 21, 41
© Planet Art, 23, 26
© Reunion des Musees Nationaux/Art Resource, NY, 20, 40
© Scala/Art Resource, NY, 13, 14, 17, 18, 29, 30, 32, 36, 37

© 2003 by KidHaven Press. KidHaven Press is an imprint of The Gale Group, Inc.,
a division of Thomson Learning, Inc.

KidHaven™ and Thomson Learning™ are trademarks used herein under license.

For more information, contact
KidHaven Press
27500 Drake Rd.
Farmington Hills, MI 48331-3535
Or you can visit our Internet site at http://www.gale.com

LIBRARY OF CONGRESS CATALOGING-IN-PUBLICATION DATA

Nardo, Don, 1947–
  The Italian Renaissance / by Don Nardo.
    p. cm. — (History of the world series)
Summary: Discusses the Renaissance period in Italian history, when ideals of
creativity and democracy as practiced in ancient Greece were revived, leading
to great advances in art, science, and other disciplines.
Includes bibliographical references and index.
  ISBN 0-7377-1036-5 (lib : alk. paper)
  1. Italy—Civilization—1268–1559—Juvenile literature. 2. Renaissance—Italy—
Juvenile literature. [1. Italy—Civilization—1268–1559. 2. Renaissance—Italy.]
I. Title. II. Series.
  DG445.N37 2003
  945'.05—dc21

                                                                    2002152133

Printed in China

Contents

Introduction
Defining the Renaissance

The European Renaissance, which lasted from about 1300 to 1600, began in Italy and had its greatest flowering there. Eventually it spread to other countries. Modern scholars have developed various definitions for the Renaissance. On the one hand, they point to the word itself, which means "rebirth." Indeed, the Renaissance was a time when educated Italians and other Europeans rediscovered the impressive civilizations of ancient Greece and Rome. They collected and studied ancient texts in the original Greek and Latin and found ideas and lessons they greatly admired. And they tried to apply these ideas and lessons to their own society.

Another way of looking at the Renaissance is as a historical period. In this view, it marked the transition between the Middle Ages, or medieval times, and the modern world. The Renaissance was therefore a period of awakening. European thinkers began to reject traditional, rigid ideas about the world and humanity's place in it and to embrace more modern ways of thinking. This included new ways of looking at religion, money and financial dealings, and how people should govern themselves.

Finally, the Renaissance was an intellectual and cultural movement. Writers and artists were inspired by the new ways that humans looked at themselves

---

This map of Renaissance Europe was created in the 1500s by an Italian, Antonio da Varese.

and their world, as well as by ancient Greek and Roman culture. So the Renaissance witnessed an immense outburst of creativity. Great literary works, magnificent paintings, and huge buildings with imposing architecture were produced, especially in Italy. Many of these creations have survived and today are viewed as classics.

It would be misleading to say that any one of these definitions for the Renaissance is more accurate than the others. All are correct. However, it is possible to make a single observation about the Italian Renaissance that fits all three. Namely, it was a time in which a few people in a tiny corner of the globe tried to change themselves for the better and in the process changed the world.

Chapter One

Italy Dominates Trade and Business

One of the chief developments of the Renaissance was a major increase in trade and business across much of Europe. Italy became the main player in Europe's expanding financial dealings. Italian merchants and bankers regulated and controlled most of the trade by the mid-1300s.

The Italians enjoyed this financial supremacy for two reasons, the first having to do with geography. Two major spheres of commerce existed in Europe in late medieval times. One was the Mediterranean Sea. It connected the ports on Europe's southern coasts to prosperous cities in Egypt, the Near East, and along the Black Sea. These eastern cities funneled products such as silks, spices, and ivory toward the west. The other commercial sphere was centered on the North Sea, including southern England, northern France, Flanders (now Belgium and the Netherlands), and Germany. The main products of this region were fish, grain, wool, and timber.

Positioned directly between these two commercial spheres, the Italian peninsula was in a favorable position. Northern Italy was particularly well off because it lay at the foot of the Alps. That allowed it to control the trading corridor that led from Italy's Mediterranean ports, through the passes of the Alps, and on toward northern European markets.

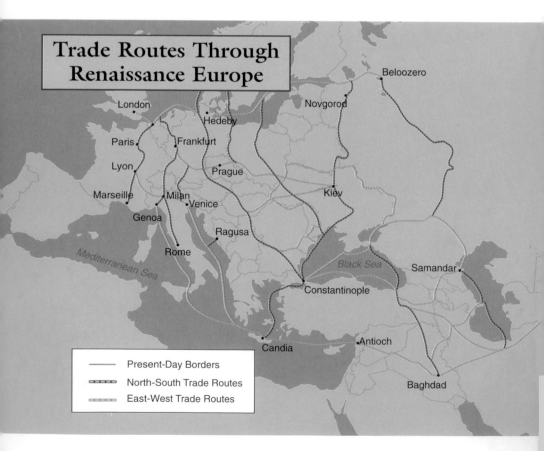

Italy's Wealth

The other reason that Italy largely controlled European trade and business was the great wealth of its individual states. At the time, Italy was not a unified nation as it is today. Instead, it was made up of several separate **city-states**. Such a state consisted of a major city surrounded by hundreds of square miles of farmland, forests, and villages, all ruled by the central city. Each state considered itself a separate nation. And there was often a fierce rivalry among the various states for economic or political dominance. Among the strongest and richest city-states were Milan, Venice, and Genoa, all in northern Italy. In central Italy the main states were Florence and the Papal States (which were ruled by the pope and had Rome as their urban center and capital).

The Merchant Class

The leading families of these states grew very wealthy from trade. Over time they also came to control most of the production processes of the goods they traded. They did this by supplying local craftsmen and laborers with raw materials such as cotton, wool, timber, and metals. For fixed wages, which the rich families largely set, the craftsmen turned out the products. The merchants then traded the goods at a much higher price. In this way, rich merchant families gained **monopolies** over many products. They also oversaw and made money from building the ships that carried the goods to distant ports.

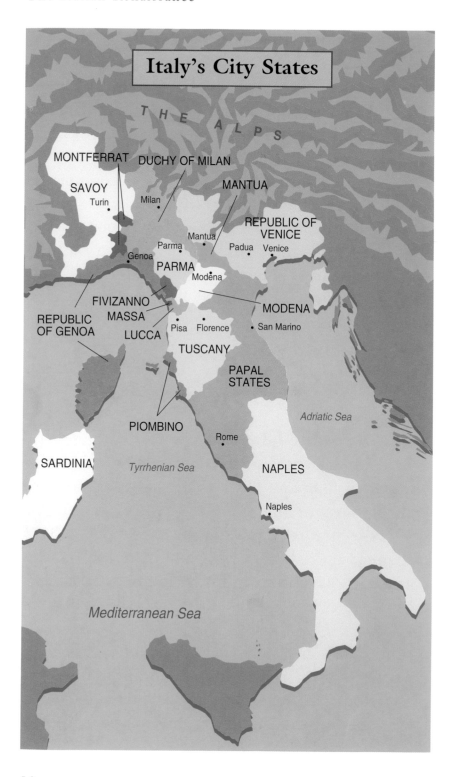

Italy's City States

THE ALPS

MONTFERRAT
DUCHY OF MILAN

SAVOY
Turin •

Milan •

MANTUA

REPUBLIC OF
VENICE

Parma •
Mantua •
Padua •
Venice •

Genoa •
PARMA
Modena •

FIVIZANNO
MASSA
MODENA

REPUBLIC
OF GENOA
LUCCA
Pisa • Florence •
San Marino •

TUSCANY

PAPAL
STATES

Adriatic Sea

PIOMBINO

Rome •

SARDINIA
Tyrrhenian Sea
NAPLES

Naples •

Mediterranean Sea

Banking was another important source of income for the rich Italian merchant families. A number of them ran banks that lent money to various merchants and nobles in both Italy and the poorer states of northern Europe. The bankers charged interest on these loans, making them even richer. In the 1400s, for example, the Medici family, based in Florence, became the main bankers in Europe. They had branches in Naples, Genoa, and Rome, as well as in London, England; the French cities of Lyon and Paris; and other cities.

Thus, immense riches flowed into Florence and other major Italian cities. Leading merchants and politicians could afford to live in large, luxurious

During the Renaissance, Italian shop owners, like these fish merchants, grew prosperous from their business.

homes and erect huge public buildings. They also hired the best artists and sculptors to decorate these structures. Visitors from other parts of Europe were amazed at the size and beauty of these cities. Venice was especially popular, with its 150 canals, 400 bridges, and numerous towering marble churches and palaces. A French traveler called it "the most triumphant city that I have ever seen."[1] And another foreigner found it "impossible to describe the beauty, magnificence, and wealth" of Venice, which had "the most beautiful [main] street in the world."[2]

International Fairs

In fact, those northern Europeans who marveled at the splendor of Venice, Florence, and other Italian cities were relatively few in number. They came from much less wealthy areas in which few people other than merchants and nobles could afford to travel. The German, French, and English towns of the era were dirty, crowded, and built of wood, **thatch**, and fieldstone. Their only contact with the glories of distant Italy was through Genoese, Venetian, and other Italian merchants. These merchants arrived each year with luxury goods to trade.

Such commerce was usually conducted in what became known as international fairs. These were gatherings of traders who met annually in various northern European locales, the first springing up in Flanders and northern France. Later, fairs were held in cities in Germany, England, and Switzerland. These gatherings lasted from one to six weeks.

Towering public buildings surround the magnificent town square in Renaissance Florence.

Merchants who attended them sometimes had to rough it, especially in backward areas like England. One Englishman wrote that the merchants "had no shelter except canvas tents; owing to the changeable gusts of wind assailing them . . . they were cold and wet, and also suffered from hunger and thirst; their feet were soiled by mud, and their goods rotted by the showers of rain."[3]

The Emergence of Credit
One practice that developed at these commercial fairs was destined to have a lasting effect on the future

A banker and his wife count their money. At left is a golden florin, an Italian coin of the period.

business dealings of the Western world. This was the emergence of **credit** as a financial tool. Credit consists of a customer owning an item and promising to pay for it later. At the fairs, coins and goods from all over Europe were used for payment. So rich Italian bankers set up tables at which they exchanged one form of currency for another. (The Italian word for such a table, *banca,* is the root of the modern word "bank.")

These bankers grew so rich they could afford to extend credit to traders who were short of cash. In such a deal, a trader signed a **promissory note**, in which he pledged to pay for the goods, plus interest, the following year. Sometimes the note and the trader's good name were enough for the banker. Other times the borrower had to put up **collateral**. The banker held onto the collateral and either returned it when the trader paid or kept it if he failed to pay. The use of credit in the Renaissance stimulated an increased volume of trade in Europe. It also helped to lay the foundations of the market economy of the modern world.

Chapter ⬤ Two

Humanism: Changes in Thinking and Learning

At the same time that the Italian city-states rose to their pivotal role in European trade and business, these states gave birth to a new intellectual movement. It was driven by a small but highly influential group of educated writers and other thinkers. They began to look at the world and the role of humans within it in new ways. This stimulated a fresh, and at the time bold, approach to education and learning. To describe this new brand of learning, a Florentine scholar, Leonardo Bruni, used the Latin word *humanitas* (meaning "humanity"). Soon this term was applied to the entire movement. It became known as "**humanism**" and its leading figures as "humanists."

Humans Shape the Limits of Nature

The movement was well named because it strongly emphasized the dignity, worth, and potential of human beings. In so doing, it went against the traditional teachings of the Church. Through most of the Middle Ages, the Church had dominated European society. Church leaders discouraged the accumulation of wealth, saying that it corrupted people. In addition, the Church dictated what behavior was moral and acceptable. It based its teachings strictly on the word of God as set down in the Bible.

The humanists argued that earlier church leaders, like St. Augustine (center), restricted people too much.

In contrast, the humanists argued that the Church restricted humans too much. It did not allow them to reach and enjoy the potential God had given them. Though wealth could indeed corrupt, they said, it could also be used to create good and noble works. Moreover, the humanists said, God had endowed

God, as pictured by a Renaissance painter. The humanists believed that God gave people free will.

people with the ability to know right from wrong. He had also given them the capacity to make reasoned choices. So a person could choose either to strive to be as good as angels or to sink to the level of pigs and other animals. And if people chose well, they might have unlimited powers to do good on Earth. Italian humanist Pico della Mirandola stated this concept in his *Oration on the Dignity of Man*. Pico has God say to the first humans: "In accordance with your free will, in whose hand We have placed you, [you] shall ordain [decide] for yourself the limits of nature."[4]

The Liberal Education

The humanists were not against either God or the Church. Indeed, most of these thinkers were devout Christians. They simply held that human virtues and values did not have to come from established religion alone.

In fact, the humanists claimed, throughout history, such **secular** values had led humanity to great heights. Thus, a strong fascination for history, especially ancient history, became a hallmark of the humanists. A Florentine, Francesco Petrarch (1304–1374), often called the father of humanism, wrote:

Among the many subjects that interested me, I dwelt especially upon **antiquity**, for our own age has almost always repelled me. . . . In order to forget my own time, I have constantly striven [tried] to place myself in spirit in other ages.[5]

A French painting depicts the ancient Greek gods. Renaissance thinkers greatly admired Greek culture.

In particular, the humanists looked back with great admiration, even awe, at the ages of ancient Greece and Rome. Greco-Roman society and culture became known as "classical" civilization. The humanists believed that classical civilization was superior to that of the Middle Ages and that much could be learned from classical thinkers. Plato and other Greeks, along with Virgil, Seneca, and other Romans, came to be seen as almost **infallible** sources of wisdom.

The works of these ancients should therefore be studied in Italian schools, the humanists insisted. In addition, they said, Greek and Roman architecture, painting, and music should be revived, imitated, and studied. Classical learning would then become a powerful civilizing force that would transform society.

The result was that Italian schools of higher learning began stressing a "liberal" education, one based on classical models. "We call those studies liberal," wrote humanist Pietro Vergerio, "which are worthy of a free man . . . that education which . . . trains and develops those highest gifts of body and mind which ennoble men."[6] Liberal courses in Italian schools included the study of history, languages, music, athletics, good manners, and moral behavior. The Bible was still studied and revered.

An Italian teacher of mathematics (center) poses proudly with one of his students.

But most members of the educated classes no longer viewed it as the primary guide for everyday life.

The Universal Man

Being individuals, the Italian humanists used their liberal educations in varied ways. Some kept to themselves or associated mainly with other scholars. Their study of the classics tended to focus on narrow topics and provided little benefit to their fellow citizens.

Other humanists felt that they should apply the knowledge they had acquired to practical endeavors that enriched their communities. Their dedication to public service became known as "civic humanism."

Often the civic humanists entered politics in an effort to improve the quality of government. For example, a scholar named Coluccio Salutati rose to the high office of chancellor in Florence in 1375. He was succeeded by Leonardo Bruni, the scholar who had called the new learning *humanitas.* These men believed that a society should be ruled by its best-educated citizens, who could use their great knowledge to guide the state in constructive ways. To rally a spirit of patriotism in Florence, for instance, Bruni composed a proud history of the city. Another civic humanist, Leon Battista Alberti (1404–1472), designed and erected great buildings in Florence.

Alberti became a model of the ideal Renaissance humanist—a highly rounded individual who mastered many areas of endeavor. In addition to being an

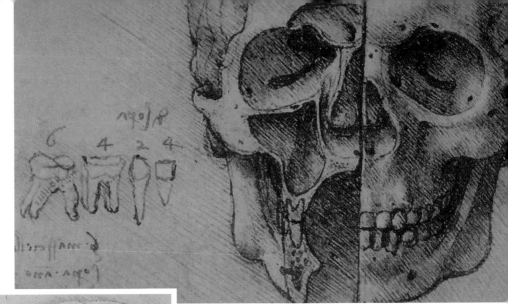

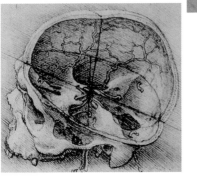

This drawing done by Leonardo in 1489 shows the outside of a human skull (top, right) and part of the interior (top, left). In another beautiful drawing completed in 1489, Leonardo depicts the inside of a human brain case (left).

architect and builder, he composed music and wrote both poetry and prose. He was also a versatile athlete who excelled at wrestling, running, high-jumping, and archery.

More famous and even more versatile and accomplished was Leonardo da Vinci. Born near Florence in 1452, he became a skilled painter and sculptor, as well as an inventor and engineer. In a letter to a prospective employer, the ruler of Milan, Leonardo offered a mere partial list of his diverse talents:

I would contrive catapults . . . and other [war] machines of marvelous efficiency and . . . in time of peace I . . . [excel] in architecture and the composition of buildings, public and private. . . . I can carry out sculpture in marble, bronze, or clay, and also I can do in painting whatever [you feel] may [need to] be done.[7]

Alberti and Leonardo were prime examples of what became known as *l'uomo universale,* the "universal man." Today, a person with many talents and skills is called a "Renaissance" man or woman. Thus, the best of the Italian humanists set an example of excellence for all future generations.

Chapter Three

Art of Unsurpassed Grandeur and Beauty

For many people, hearing the word Renaissance immediately brings to mind great accomplishments in the arts. Indeed, that period witnessed an incredible outburst of artistic creativity. The painters, sculptors, and architects of the Italian Renaissance produced works that set standards of excellence for Western culture for centuries to come.

The remarkable achievement of these artists is perhaps best seen in the area of painting. Prior to the Renaissance, Italian and other European painting was largely a tool used by the Church. Most ordinary people in medieval times could not read. So a priest or other educated person read the Bible to them. To help

The Greek hero Perseus fights a monster in this painting by the Italian master Piero di Cosimo.

the listeners better visualize biblical figures and events, churchmen had artists do illustrations. Each picture was meant to present an important idea or teach a moral lesson. Such works were generally **two-dimensional**, or flat-looking, and not very realistic.

In contrast, the painters of the Renaissance believed that art could and should have other uses. For example, although religious events and themes remained prominent subjects for painters, they also glorified the secular world. This included the beauties and wonders of nature, including the naked human body. As was the case with literature, Renaissance artists were influenced by classical models. So many paintings now included

pagan gods and heroes of Greek and Roman mythology. Also, Renaissance artists devoted years to developing their technical skills. They learned to draw and paint bodies and objects in their proper proportions, in different kinds of light, and in realistic detail. As a result, their canvases seemed three-dimensional and filled with energy and drama.

Giotto Introduces Realism

Historians often divide the development of Italian Renaissance art into three broad periods. The first, spanning the early 1300s, was dominated by Giotto di Bondone (1266–1336), who later became known as the father of Renaissance painting. A native of Florence,

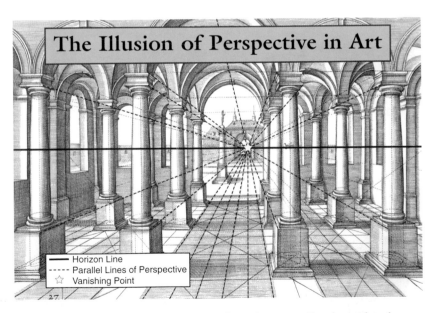

The Illusion of Perspective in Art

Horizon Line
- - - - Parallel Lines of Perspective
☆ Vanishing Point

Renaissance artists create the illusion of perspective in art by drawing a series of lines beginning with the horizon line. Next they add parallel lines, which come together at a vanishing point, the point where all of the lines meet on the horizon line. When combined the piece of art has a three-dimensional appearance.

Giotto also worked for long periods in other Italian cities, including Padua and Naples. The famous Renaissance artist and biographer Giorgio Vasari said of him: "Although born amidst incapable artists and at a time when all good methods in art had long been entombed [in the ruins of Greece and Rome] . . . [he] alone succeeded in restoring [art] to a path that may be called the true one."[8]

The "true path" was one on which art broke free of the medieval style, with its flat, lifeless, unrealistic depiction of people and objects. Giotto's human figures seemed to have thickness and weight. Moreover, he placed them in settings that created the illusion of space, depth, and distance.

Another first for Giotto was capturing human emotions in art, something medieval artists had not attempted. His great **fresco** adorning the inside of the Arena Chapel in Padua is an excellent example. The work depicts various episodes in the life of Christ. Giotto makes the human figures display their moods and feelings through subtle, realistic facial expressions and hand gestures.

Old Forms Reach New Heights

Giotto's work strongly influenced the leaders of the second major period in Renaissance art, which began in the early 1400s. Another Florentine, Tommaso Guidi Masaccio (1401–1428), reached new levels of realism in works such as *Expulsion from Paradise* and *Christ and the Tribute Money*. Masaccio's last painting, *The Holy Trinity*, is particularly striking. It depicts the altar

This fresco, titled *St. Francis and the Skeleton,* was created by an unknown follower of Giotto.

section of a chapel, with pillars, walls, and ceilings that create the illusion of a real physical space.

Masaccio only painted architecture. But the real thing reached new heights in the hands of his countryman, Filippo Brunelleschi (1377–1446). "It may be said," Vasari wrote of Brunelleschi, "that he was given by heaven to invest architecture with new forms, after it had wandered astray for many centuries."[9] The "new form" Brunelleschi created was actually a new version of an older form. He was inspired by the classical style of architecture used by the Romans.

In particular, Brunelleschi admired the huge dome of the Pantheon, an impressive Roman structure that had survived intact. After studying this ancient marvel, he tackled the seemingly impossible job of creating a dome 138 feet across and 133 feet high for Florence's cathedral. The task was completed in 1434. This and

Brunelleschi (right) shows a model of a cathedral to the wealthy man paying for its construction.

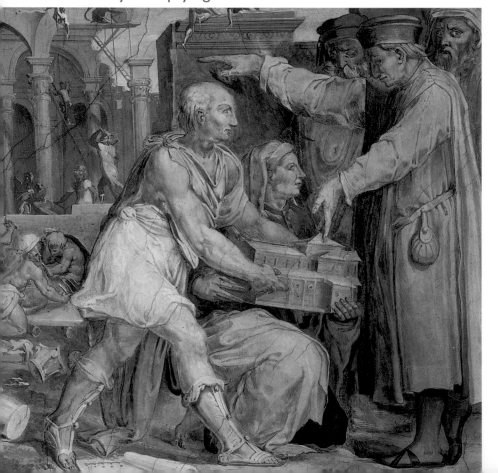

other architectural feats by Brunelleschi became models followed by later Renaissance architects, including the great Michelangelo.

The Height of Renaissance Art

Michelangelo Buonarroti (1475–1564) was the supreme artist of the Renaissance. A painter, sculptor, and architect of immense talent, some experts call him the greatest artist ever produced by Western civilization. He and two other masters, Leonardo da Vinci and Raphael (Raffaello Sanzio, 1483–1520), dominated the third major period of Renaissance art. It lasted from the late 1400s through the early 1500s.

As an architect, Michelangelo followed in Brunelleschi's footsteps by borrowing columns, domes, and other structural forms from the Romans. And it was in Rome that Michelangelo's greatest buildings rose. The most famous is St. Peter's Basilica, of which he designed the dome and several other sections. The dome is 138 feet wide and its top towers 452 feet above street level.

Michelangelo's architectural work was surpassed only by his efforts in sculpture and painting. His magnificent statue of *David,* created between 1501 and 1504, stands fourteen feet high and seems almost to breathe with life. Michelangelo believed that a finished sculpture lay trapped within a block of marble. It only remained for the artist to help it escape. "In hard and craggy stone," he said, "the mere removal of the surface gives being to a figure, which ever grows the more the stone is **hewn** away." [10]

This is a detail from Michelangelo's *Last Judgment,* a fresco that covers the ceiling of the Sistine Chapel.

Perhaps the most famous of all Michelangelo's works is his vast series of frescoes painted on the ceiling of the Sistine Chapel, in the Vatican in Rome. The paintings, completed between 1508 and 1512, depict the creation of the universe. The most famous shows God endowing the first human, Adam, with the spark of life. A great scholar once called the Sistine Chapel ceiling "the greatest achievement of any man in the history of painting."[11] Few would argue with this view. Nor can it be denied that, for grandeur and beauty, the art of Italy's Renaissance has only occasionally been equaled and never surpassed.

Chapter Four

The Renaissance Spreads to Northern Europe

Although the Renaissance began and long flourished in Italy, it eventually influenced cultural developments in northern Europe. Humanist ideas, fascination with Greek and Roman culture, and artistic concepts and styles spread northward in different ways. Italy had earned a reputation as Europe's most **prestigious** center of learning. So during the 1400s and 1500s growing numbers of well-to-do families in Germany, France, England, and other northern countries sent their sons to be educated in Italy. These students later returned home with new and influential ideas. Merchants who traveled back and forth from Italy to northern Europe also helped to spread such ideas.

From Florence (pictured) and other Italian cities the Renaissance spread to northern Europe.

Even more crucial in this process was the appearance of large numbers of affordable printed books in the second half of the fifteenth century. In the 1440s a German named Johannes Gutenberg invented the printing press. Before this, northern Europe had only limited access to a few hand-written copies of the works of the classical authors and Italian humanists. However, the new printing technology spread rapidly. By 1500 more than twenty-five hundred European cities had their own presses. And by 1517 most of the works of the ancient Roman writers were in print. Also, the 1500s witnessed an increasing number of classical and Italian works undergo translation into northern

European tongues, including English. This made these writings available to increasing numbers of people.

The northern Europeans had their own unique reactions to these works. Like many Italian Renaissance thinkers, scholars in the north often challenged local churchmen with new ways of looking at things. However, in the north there was a stronger emphasis on religious reform. In particular, northern European humanists felt that the Church had lost the purity it had possessed in its early centuries. They wanted to see the clergy pay less attention to elaborate ceremonies and more attention to simple good works.

The printing press made many famous books, including Dante's *Divine Comedy,* available to a wide audience.

The Northern Humanists

This northern European brand of humanism was most clearly expressed by a Dutchman named Desiderius Erasmus (1466–1536). He pointed out certain similarities in the teachings of Christ and those of a number of ancient classical thinkers. He felt that no one had taught the importance of leading an upright, moral life better than Christ. "Nevertheless," he added,

> one may find in the books of the pagans [i.e., the Greeks and Romans] very much which does agree with it. . . . According to [the Greek thinker]

Plato and Aristotle (at center) are among the Greek thinkers depicted in Raphael's *School of Athens.*

Plato, [his teacher] Socrates says . . . that a wrong must not be repaid with a wrong. . . . And [the Greek philosopher] Aristotle has written . . . that nothing can be a delight to us . . . except virtue. If there be things that belong particularly to Christianity in these ancient writers, let us follow them. [12]

Erasmus therefore promoted studying both the Bible and ancient philosophy as a way of strengthening basic Christian values.

More Greek thinkers are pictured in this detail (lower right) of the *School of Athens.*

Italian humanism also began to filter into England in the late 1400s and early 1500s. After studying in Italy, John Colet became dean of St. Paul's Cathedral in London and in 1510 founded St. Paul's school. He broke with tradition in appointing the headmaster. Instead of a priest, he chose a humanist scholar, John Lily. Colet also insisted that the students learn to read and write Latin and Greek and study the works of the ancient authors.

Colet knew and influenced the greatest of the English Renaissance humanists—Sir Thomas More

The Dutch thinker Erasmus was the most important of the northern humanists.

(1478–1535). Together with Lily and Erasmus, More translated several ancient Greek works into Latin. And like Erasmus, More tried to use "pure" and "noble" classical ideas to reform religion and society, which he felt had grown corrupt.

Northern Artists

Northern Europe also felt the influence of the Italian Renaissance in the arts. Flemish painters had strong contacts with Italy beginning in the late 1400s. For example, Quentin Massys and Jan Gossaert, both of Flanders, were inspired by Leonardo da Vinci. Massys adopted da Vinci's style of portrait painting, which stressed realism and natural facial expressions. A fine example of Massys's work is his portrait of Erasmus, painted for the writer's friend, Sir Thomas More.

Meanwhile, in Germany the leading figure of Renaissance art was Albrecht Dürer (1471–1528). He was as skilled at engraving pictures on wood as painting them on canvas. Two extended visits to Italy (1494–1495 and 1505–1507) proved pivotal in developing his style. After he had studied the work of Italian masters up close, his paintings became bolder and more realistic. One of Dürer's greatest works is the *Adoration of the Trinity,* completed in 1511. It shows God, Christ, and the Holy Ghost, with numerous saints and angels posed in separate groups around them. This general format is similar to that employed by Michelangelo in his great painting in the Sistine Chapel.

England's Theatrical Renaissance

Humanism and art were not the only aspects of the Italian Renaissance that influenced northern Europe in the sixteenth century. During the reign of Queen Elizabeth I (1558–1603), England produced a golden age of theater and drama. Some aspects of this achievement developed from native English theatrical traditions. But a considerable number of ideas were borrowed from Italian plays and classical plays that the Italians had revived.

In particular, English playwrights felt the influence of the Roman playwright Seneca. Seneca's tragedies were rediscovered in Italy in the mid-1500s. Almost immediately, English playwrights began to copy their style. Seneca drew most of his characters from classical myths and legends and dealt with serious, weighty themes such as murder and revenge. Also, many characters died in his plays (though always offstage).

A major turning point in the development of this style was *The Spanish Tragedy* (ca. 1586), by Thomas Kyd. It was the first example of a popular kind of drama known as the "revenge play." All revenge plays featured a hero seeking bloody justice against one or more **villains** who had wronged him.

A portrait of the English playwright William Shakespeare.

The greatest playwright of the Elizabethan Age, William Shakespeare (1564–1616), wrote revenge plays of his own. One was *Hamlet,* one of the two or three finest tragedies ever written. The story concerns the troubles of the title character, who is a royal prince of Denmark. He seeks revenge against his uncle, who had killed his father and stolen the throne.

The play, along with others by Shakespeare and his

Hamlet's friend, Ophelia, drowns in a stream in Shakespeare's famous revenge play, *Hamlet.*

colleagues, shows the influence of the Italian Renaissance in other ways. For example, a number of lines and speeches reflect humanist views of the dignity and worth of human beings. "What a piece of work is a man!" Hamlet says. "How noble in reason! How infinite in faculties [abilities]! In form and moving how express and admirable! In action how like an angel!" [13] This is how the ancient Greeks had seen humans. Their enlightened views of the world had been lost for many centuries until the Italian Renaissance revived them. The Elizabethan writers and others then passed them on to the modern world. The great wheel of Western culture has come full circle.

Notes

Chapter One: Italy Dominates Trade and Business

1. Quoted in Will Durant, *The Renaissance*. New York: Simon and Schuster, 1953, p. 281.
2. Quoted in Pompeo Melneti, *Venice*. Boston: Murray, 1907, vol. 2, p. 62.
3. Quoted in Leon Bernard and Theodore B. Hodges, eds., *Readings in European History*. New York: Macmillan, 1958, p. 116.

Chapter Two: Humanism: Changes in Thinking and Learning

4. Quoted in Ernst Cassirier et al, eds., *The Renaissance Philosophy of Man*. Chicago: Phoenix, 1961, p. 224.
5. Quoted in Frederic A. Ogg, ed., *A Source Book of Medieval History*. New York: American Book, 1908, pp. 472–73.
6. Quoted in De Lamar Jensen, *Renaissance Europe: Age of Recovery and Reconciliation*. Lexington, MA: D.C. Heath, 1981, p. 111.
7. Quoted in Elizabeth G. Holt, ed., *Literary Sources of Art History*. Princeton: Princeton University Press, 1947, p. 170.

Chapter Three: Art of Unsurpassed Grandeur and Beauty

8. Giorgio Vasari, *Lives of the Most Eminent Painters, Sculptors, and Architects,* trans. Mrs. Jonathan

Foster. London: Henry G. Bohn, 1855, vol. 1, p. 93.

9. Vasari, *Lives,* vol. 2, p. 270.
10. Quoted in J.A. Symonds, *Life of Michelangelo Buonarotti,* 1893; reprint. Philadelphia: University of Pennsylvania Press, 2002, p. 70.
11. Durant, *Renaissance,* p. 475.

Chapter Four: The Renaissance Spreads to Northern Europe

12. Quoted in John C. Olin, ed. and trans., *Christian Humanism and the Reformation: Desiderius.* New York: Harper, 1965, p. 101.
13. William Shakespeare, *Hamlet,* act 2, scene 2, lines 319–21.

Glossary

antiquity: Ancient times.

city-state: A small country consisting of a major central city surrounded by supporting villages and farms.

collateral: A piece of property given by a borrower to a lender to secure a loan. The lender returns the collateral when the loan is paid.

credit: In a financial deal, when a customer takes possession of an item and promises to pay the seller later.

fresco: A painting done on wet plaster. The paint dries with the plaster and becomes part of the wall.

hewn: Chopped or carved.

humanism: An intellectual movement that emerged in northern Italy during the Renaissance. It stressed secular values, the worth of dignity of human beings, and the grandeur of ancient Greek and Roman culture.

infallible: Unerring; or incapable of making mistakes.

monopoly: Sole control of something.

pagan: Non-Christian.

prestigious: Famous, important, and having an excellent reputation.

promissory note: A written document in which a borrower promises to pay back a loan.

secular: Nonspiritual.

thatch: A primitive kind of building material made up of bundled twigs or plant stems.

two-dimensional: Flat-looking.

villain: A bad or disreputable person or character.

For Further Exploration

Alison Cole, *Renaissance*. London: Dorling Kindersley, 2000. Like all of Dorling Kindersley's books, this one is lavishly illustrated and nicely captures the look of the Renaissance while offering a general overview of the period.

Andrew Langley, *Leonardo and His Times*. New York: Dorling Kindersley, 2000. An informative, very colorfully illustrated volume covering the life and accomplishments of one of the greatest geniuses who ever lived.

——, *Shakespeare's Theater*. New York: Oxford University Press, 1999. Highlighted by many eye-catching illustrations, this book is an effective guide to the Globe and other theaters of Elizabethan London, an important center of the northern Renaissance.

Vicki Leon, *Outrageous Women of the Renaissance*. Hoboken, NJ: John Wiley, 1999. Women are often left out of discussions of the Renaissance, a shortcoming admirably made up for in this delightful book. Covered are the achievements of military leader Joan of Arc, painter Elisabetta Sirani, Sweden's Queen Christina, and more.

Jacqueline Morley, *A Renaissance Town*. New York: Peter Bedrik, 1996. A commendable overview of the history and culture of Florence, one of the main centers of the Italian Renaissance.

Robert G. Shearer, *Famous Men of the Renaissance and Reformation*. Lebanon, TN: Greenleaf Press, 1996. Presents short biographies of several of the more important figures of the Renaissance.

Diane Stanley, *Michelangelo*. New York: Harper-Collins, 2000. This brief but well-written biography of the great Renaissance man Michelangelo also includes many handsome illustrations and some excellent background information about the period.

Index